JOE KEATINGE
DAN SLOTT (ASM #699.1)
WRITERS

RICHARD ELSON
(MORBIUS #1-5, 8-9)
VALENTINE DE LANDRO
(ASM #699.1, MORBIUS #6-7)
CARLOS RODRIGUEZ (MORBIUS #5)
FELIX RUIZ (MORBIUS #7)
MARCO CHECCHETTO
(ASM #699.1)
ARTISTS

ANTONIO FABELA
COLOURS

FABIO CIACCI
LETTERING

STEPHEN WACKER
SANA AMANAT
ELLIE PYLE
DEVIN LEWIS
EDITORIAL

C.B. CEBULSKI
EDITOR IN CHIEF

SPIDER-MAN created by **STAN LEE**
& **STEVE DITKO**

MORBIUS
THE LIVING VAMPIRE
MIDNIGHT SON

Chief Executive Officer: Aldo H. Sallustro. Publishing Director Europe: Marco M. Lupoi. Licensing: Annalisa Califano and Beatrice Doti. Editorial Coordinator: Ilaria Tavoni. Art Director: Mario Corticelli. Graphic Design: Antonio D'Achille. Repro packaging: Mario Da Rin Zanco, Valentina Esposito, Luca Ficarelli, Linda Leporati. Pre-press: Cristina Bedini & Andrea Lusoli.

INTRO

Who is **Michael Morbius**? A Nobel-Prize winning scientist, an outsider, someone who wants to do good in the world but can't… because of his insatiable thirst for blood! He's no hero, but he's not exactly a criminal either – like **Curt Connors** AKA the **Lizard**, he's a victim of his own scientific ambitions, and isn't in control of himself when he kills. Horrified by his transformation, he considers himself an abomination, but has fought to protect his own 'kind' in the **Legion of Monsters**, a menagerie of Marvel monstrosities including **Manphibian**, **the Living Mummy**, and **Werewolf by Night**. Morbius was later recruited by **A.R.M.O.R.** in his capacity as an expert in biological threats to combat a plague of extradimensional zombies. He even went undercover to help his fellow scientist, **Max Modell** of Horizon Labs, to develop a cure for the spider-power virus that threatened Manhattan. Unfortunately, his blood-lust got the better of him, and it was revealed that he'd also been using his lab access to find a solution to his condition, as well at the Lizard's. Because of **Spidey**, Morbius was then locked up in the Raft maximum security prison. Now the wall-crawler has to ask the Living Vampire for help! But it's not **Peter Parker** looking for a favour – it's **Doctor Octopus**, inhabiting Pete's body as the **Superior Spider-Man**…

THE ORIGIN OF MORBIUS

Amazing Spider-Man (1999) #699.1
Cover by **STEFANO CASELLI**

A QUESTION THAT HAS VEXED ME MY ENTIRE LIFE.

Nafplio, Greece.

YEARS AGO.

WHERE DO YOU THINK YOU'RE GOING?

EVER TIMID.

MAMA... EMIL AND I WANTED TO...

SPEAK UP, MICHAEL!

EVER UNSURE.

I THOUGHT MAYBE IT WOULD BE FUN IF I COULD GO OUTSIDE AND--

OUTSIDE? MICHAEL!

HOW MANY TIMES HAVE WE TALKED ABOUT THIS?!

AND DEFINITELY NOT MY MOTHER'S SON.

THERE'S NOTHING FOR YOU OUTSIDE! GO UPSTAIRS AND READ!

AND I DON'T WANT YOU PLAYING WITH EMIL ANYMORE!

BUT THERE WAS ALWAYS MY FATHER.

MAKARIOA MORBIUS.

FAMED SURREALIST AUTHOR, PAINTER AND FILMMAKER.

KNOWN FOR MAKING THE UNKNOWN KNOWN. NOT KNOWN FOR RAISING ME.

I DON'T EVER RECALL SEEING HIM IN PERSON.

HE MERELY EXISTED AS A MEMORY I NEVER HAD.

SOMEDAY, MICHAEL--YOU'LL UNDERSTAND.

YOU'RE TOO FRAGILE FOR THE OUTSIDE WORLD.

IN THE END I THINK HIS ABSENCE HAD AN EVEN BIGGER EFFECT ON MY MOTHER.

SHE BURIED HER LONELINESS IN OUR FAMILY BOOKSTORE, WORKING RELENTLESSLY AS MY GRANDFATHER KEPT WATCH OVER HIS "UNWANTED DAUGHTER."

ΑΝΟΙΧΤΟ

SHE CHANGED--EVER SO DRAMATICALLY.

EXCEPT FOR THE BOOKS.

WE ALWAYS HAD THE BOOKS. SO, SO MANY BOOKS.

JUST STAY IN AND READ, MICHAEL.

YOU'LL BE HAPPIER FOR IT.

MOST TIMES IT WAS FOR THE BEST.

I WAS ALWAYS HAPPIEST WHEN WE SNUCK AWAY.

AW, COME ON, MICHAEL. CLIMB UP ALREADY.

WHAT'RE YOU WORRIED ABOUT? WHAT'S THE WORST THAT COULD HAPPEN?

FALLING. FALLING COULD HAPPEN. FALLING HURTS.

SO, WHAT? I'M CONSTANTLY FALLING DOWN.

YOU GET USED TO IT AFTER A WHILE.

DON'T BE SUCH A WUSS.

I'M NOT I-- FINE.

MY CONDITION KEPT ME HESISTANT.

JUST FORGET IT.

HELP ME UP.

IT WAS RARE...AND IT WAS LETHAL.

INSIDE ME, BLOOD CELLS WERE DYING EVER SINCE I WAS BORN.

THEY RENEWED ONLY ENOUGH TO KEEP ME ALIVE.

DON'T WORRY ABOUT BALANCE-- RUN LIKE IT'S THE SIDEWALK, JUMP AT THE GAP!

O-OKAY...

BUT NOT ENOUGH TO DO ALL THE THINGS I WANTED.

I WAS YOUNG AND THE FUTURE WAS IN FRONT OF ME. WIDE AND OPEN.

YOU'LL BE FINE! JUST LEAP!

GO, MICHAEL!

EVERYTHING ABOUT MY WORLD WAS A LIFE-AFFIRMING RISK...

MOTHER DIDN'T TAKE IT LIGHTLY.

BUT EVEN SHE WAS SYMPATHETIC.

YOU'RE NOT LIKE OTHER BOYS, MICHAEL.

YOU NEED TO STAY INSIDE.

AND, EMIL, TRUE FRIEND THAT HE WAS...UNDERSTOOD.

I AM SO, SO, SO SORRY. I--I HAD NO IDEA.

IT WON'T HAPPEN TO YOU AGAIN.

I'LL MAKE GOOD ON THIS, I PROMISE.

HE REALLY DID MAKE GOOD.

NOT MANY FRIENDS BASE THEIR PROFESSIONS ON A CHILDHOOD PROMISE.

YESTERDAY'S DATA WAS QUITE POSITIVE, MICHAEL.

THE BAT'S BLOOD LEVELS WERE RISING. I THINK WE MAY FINALLY HAVE SOMETHING.

THAT'S CERTAINLY A WELCOME CHANGE.

GOOD MORNING, DARLINGS.

READY TO TRY CURING OUR DEAR MICHAEL AGAIN?

DON'T ANTAGONIZE THEM.

WELL, IT'S STILL LOOKING CONFUSING.

WE'VE DETERMINED YOUR BLOOD CELLS ARE... DYING? CONSTANTLY? I'M NOT SURE HOW ELSE TO LOOK AT IT.

BUT THERE'S SO MUCH THAT DOESN'T MAKE SENSE ABOUT-- WAIT A SEC.

EVERYTHING OKAY?

WOW.

YEAH, MICHAEL-- EVERYTHING IS VERY "OKAY."

IT'S YOUR BLOOD LEVELS.

THEY'RE ACTUALLY UP.

I THINK THE VAMPIRE BAT SERUM IS WORKING.

STILL, WE'LL NEED TO DO A LOT MORE ANIMAL TESTING BEFORE WE CAN MOVE ON TO FULL HUMAN TRIALS.

THIS IS A GREAT START.

YEARS IN THE MAKING.

PROBABLY YEARS LEFT TO GO.

SURE, BUT--I THINK IT'S MORE THAN WE IMAGINED. I THINK WE'RE ONTO SOMETHING BIG.

REAL BIG.

NOBEL PRIZE BIG.

AND IT WAS.

YOU SHOULD HAVE GONE, MICHAEL! THE NOBEL CEREMONY WAS GLORIOUS!

THE FOOD! THE WINE! THE LARGE CHECK WE RECEIVED!

SEE THIS TEACUP, EMIL?

IT'S A VISIBLE TEA CUP, YES.

WHY?

LOOK AT MY HAND.

GOOD LORD. THAT IS DISGUSTING.

WHAT HAPPENED?

THE TEA CUP HAPPENED.

I LIFTED IT UP AND WITH MY BLOOD AND BONE BEHAVING THE WAY THEY DO...

"SNAP."

NOW DO YOU SEE WHY I WASN'T UP FOR A CEREMONY?

I DON'T IMAGINE I WOULD HAVE FARED BETTER WITH WINE.

A POINT WELL MADE.

IN THE END, THE RESULT'S STILL THE SAME.

THE CHECK'S CLEARED, I TAKE IT?

IT ABSOLUTELY HAS.

THE WAIT IS OVER.

WE CAN FINALLY CURE YOU, MICHAEL.

WE CAN FINALLY CURE EVERYONE.

THEN THERE WAS MARTINE.

THE ONE CONSISTENTLY BRIGHT SPOT DURING AN OTHERWISE DARK TIME.

I DON'T BELIEVE THE NOBEL COMMITTEE EXPECTED YOU TO BUY A YACHT, DEAR.

IT'S A RENTAL.

BESIDES, THE REASONING'S PURELY SCIENTIFIC.

IS IT NOW?

HAVE YOU EVER KNOWN ME TO BE ONE FOR EXTRAVAGANCE, MARTINE?

IF I COULD DO THIS IN MY LIVING ROOM, I'D PREFER IT.

NOW I BELIEVE YOU.

I'M NOT SURE HOW I FELL FOR SUCH A RECLUSE.

I CAN'T SAY I FOLLOW YOU THERE EITHER.

AN OUT AND ABOUT SOCIETY GIRL FALLS FOR A MOROSE SCIENTIST WHO CAN'T STAND THE SUN?

I DON'T EVEN HAVE A HYPOTHESIS FOR THAT ONE.

A "HYPOTHESIS."

MICHAEL, MICHAEL, MICHAEL...

...NEVER CHANGE.

I DON'T PLAN TO.

I'M ASSUMING YOU DO HAVE SOME *"HYPOTHESIS"* FOR THE BOAT?

FOR THE EXPERIMENT, YES.

IT'S... COMPLICATED.

EMIL AND I COULDN'T DO THIS ON LAND.

ALL TOO DANGEROUS FOR US LAND DWELLERS?

SOMETHING LIKE THAT, YES. THE LESS YOU KNOW, THE BETTER.

I DON'T WANT TO WORRY YOU.

WORRY? MICHAEL, I HAVE NOTHING BUT FAITH IN WHAT YOU'RE DOING.

IF THERE'S ANYTHING I'VE LEARNED ABOUT YOU...

...YOU ALWAYS DO THE RIGHT THING.

I TRIED TO, ANYWAY.

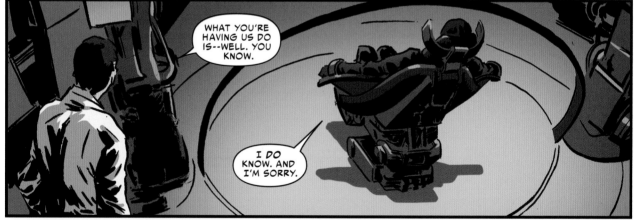

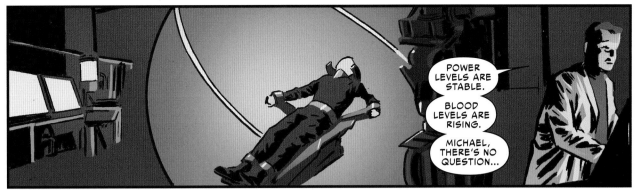

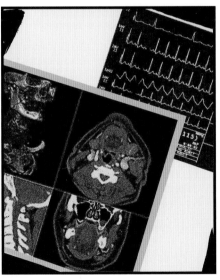

I NEVER HAD THOSE *"MOST TIMES"* AGAIN.

W-WHAT HAVE I DONE?

WHAT HAVE I BECOME?

ANY INNOCENCE IN ME WAS GONE WITH EMIL AND WHAT I HAD DONE TO HIM.

MEMORIES I HAD, NOW LOST. FORGOTTEN.

EVERYTHING WAS GONE IN AN INSTANT.

YEARS OF PREPARATION TORN APART BY MY OWN HASTE.

IF THIS COULD HAPPEN TO HIM--THEN MARTINE...

I CAN'T STAY HERE.

SHE'LL COME AND--

I HAD TO...

YOU'LL BE FINE! JUST LEAP!

...GO.

IT HASN'T BEEN EASY. MY OLD DISEASE WAS REPLACED BY A WORSE CONDITION.

A BLOODLUST.

IT'S GIVEN ME ENEMIES.

NOW, LIKE I SAID, MORBIUS--

THE LIZARD AND I PLAN TO HELP YOU--

--WHETHER YOU LIKE IT OR NOT!

THE FEW ALLIES I FOUND WERE AS BROKEN AND TWISTED AS I WAS.

ALL REFLECTIONS OF THE MONSTER I'VE BECOME.

WHAMM

USUALLY MEN NOBLER THAN ME, TRYING TO RIGHTFULLY PUT ME DOWN.

YET, I ALWAYS RESISTED.

ALWAYS FOUGHT AGAINST THEM DOING WHAT SHOULD BE DONE.

WELL... MICHAEL?

I ASK AGAIN...WHERE DO YOU THINK YOU'RE GOING?

HORIZON LABS.

MY CURE'S STILL THERE, I COULD--

REMINDERS OF WHAT HUMANITY I HAD LONG LOST.

REMINDERS OF WHAT I SHOULD LEAVE CAGED.

THE CURE?! HA!

EVERY LAST DROP WAS USED ON ME AND LOOK HOW THAT TURNED OUT!

YOU'RE REMAINING A MONSTER, MORBIUS!

"WHAT DO YOU PLAN TO DO NOW?!"

I KNOW HE'S RIGHT.

THERE'S NOWHERE TO GO NOW. NO ONE TO TURN TO.

THERE'S NO HOPE AT HORIZON. NO HOME LEFT IN GREECE.

THERE'S ONLY THE WORLD MY MOTHER WARNED ME OF, WITH ALL THE DANGERS IT BRINGS.

I WANT A COMPLETE CLEAN SWEEP OF THE AREA! DAMAGE TO THE RAFT HAS BEEN EXTENSIVE!

REPORTS SHOW WE'RE MISSING SEVERAL INMATES, INCLUDING OTTO OCTAVIUS!

I ALSO WANT TOTAL CONFIRMATION THE FOLLOWING INMATES ARE STILL IMPRISONED.

ALISTAIR SMYTHE!

CURT CONNORS!

THOSE WHO WOULD IMPRISON ME. THOSE WHO WOULD TAKE MY LIFE.

THOSE LIKE THE SPIDER-MAN, THE OCTOPUS, THE POLICE...

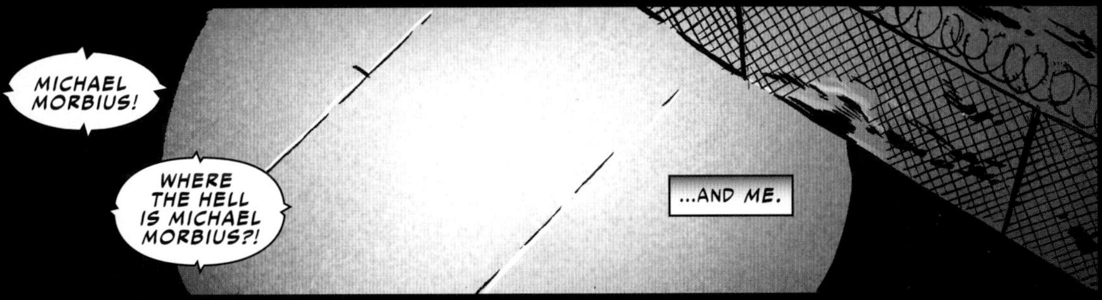
MICHAEL MORBIUS!
WHERE THE HELL IS MICHAEL MORBIUS?!
...AND ME.

MIDNIGHT SON

Morbius: The Living Vampire (2013) #1
Cover by **GABRIELE DELL'OTTO**

I WAS A LIVING VAMPIRE.

I DON'T SLEEP ANYMORE.

I DON'T MEAN I'M AN INSOMNIAC.

I DON'T MEAN I'M RESTLESS UNTIL 2 A.M., CLICKING THROUGH CHANNEL AFTER CHANNEL BECAUSE I'M STRESSED ABOUT MY BILLS.

I MEAN I AM *ALWAYS* AWAKE.

ALWAYS ALWAYS.

AS IN I HAVEN'T SHUT MY EYES TO SLEEP FOR A WHILE NOW.

AS IN I DON'T EVEN REMEMBER DREAMS ANYMORE.

KLIK-KLAK

SO, YES, I NEVER, EVER SLEEP.

BUT LUCKILY FOR ME, NEITHER DOES THIS CITY.

BLAM

BEING ABLE TO GET AROUND WITHOUT NEEDING TO SLEEP IS ONE OF THE FEW ADVANTAGES OF BEING VAMPIRE-ISH.

ADVANTAGES OF BEING VAMPIRE-ISH:

PRETTY STRONG.

KRNKK

PRETTY STRONGER THAN MOST, ANYWAY.

MOSTLY IMPERVIOUS.

COME ON... HURRY UP...

(HEALING HAS ITS LIMITS.)

CAN MORE OR LESS HYPNOTIZE PEOPLE.

OR, AT LEAST, STRONGLY SUGGEST.

GONNA NEED TO BORROW YOUR COAT.

PLEASE.

UH-- SURE.

TRANSVECTION.

I.E., GLIDING A BIT.

DISADVANTAGES OF BEING VAMPIRE-ISH:

MODERN MYTHS OF THE MODERN VAMPIRE:

I AM NOT A VAMPIRE.

I AM NOT A SUPER VILLAIN.

I AM NOT A SUPER HERO.

MY NAME IS MICHAEL MORBIUS.
I WAS A LIVING VAMPIRE...
BOOM
NOW, I'M A DEAD MAN.

BEFORE ALL THIS.

Barretto Point.
FIVE DAYS AGO.

WHERE THE HELL...

BELIEVE IT OR NOT...

...THERE ONCE WAS A TIME BEFORE MY CHEST EXPLODED.

YOU'RE NOT LIKE OTHER BOYS, MICHAEL.

YES, WAY BACK THEN.

BUT ALSO SEVERAL DAYS AGO.

...DID YOU COME FROM?

LONG STORY.

WHEN I FIRST TOOK MY LEAVE OF ABSENCE...

YOU ALL RIGHT?

I'M ACTUALLY FREEZING.

...FROM PRISON.*

YOU DON'T HAPPEN TO HAVE AN EXTRA STASH OF CLOTHES ANYWHERE, DO YOU?

*SEE AMAZING SPIDER-MAN #699.1 FOR THE WHOLE STORY.

YOU'RE GONNA WANT TO FIND SOME BETTER FITTING CLOTHES, MAN.

THEY'LL WORK FOR NOW.

THANK YOU, JUSTIN.

MAN. CLOTHES ARE THE LEAST OF YOUR PROBLEMS.

SOUNDS LIKE YOU GOTTA GET THE HELL OUT OF NEW YORK. PRETTY SURE THAT PRISON OF YOURS WANTS YOU BACK.

I CAN'T LEAVE.

NOT YET.

I NEED TO TAKE CARE OF A FEW THINGS.

WELL, THEN LAY LOW FOR A WHILE. AND NOT IN MANHATTAN.

TOO MANY DAMN SUPER HEROES IN MANHATTAN.

SO, GO SOMEWHERE THEY DON'T GO.

LIKE WHERE?

LIKE BROWNSVILLE.

FOR THE MOST PART, SUPER HEROES NEVER EVEN HEARD OF BROWNSVILLE.

SOUNDS PERFECT.

YEAH. "PERFECT."

TELL THAT TO THE PEOPLE THAT HAVE TO LIVE THERE.

IT'S NOT JUST THE SUPER HEROES LETTING IT ROT.

IT'S THE PEOPLE LIVING THERE. IT'S THE COPS.

IT'S ANYONE WHO COULD DO ANYTHING ABOUT ANYTHING.

AT *BEST* YOU GET SOME ROOKIES FORCED ON THE BEAT, MAYBE BEING TRAINED BY A VETERAN WHO LEARNED TO NOT GIVE A DAMN.

YOU'LL SEE.

I HOPE YOU WERE AT THAT SUPER-PRISON 'CAUSE YOU'RE SUPER-JACKED. IT'S A GOOD PLACE TO LAY LOW, BUT, WELL--

LET'S STICK TO "YOU'LL SEE."

SWEAT IT WHEN YOU GET THERE.

HEY, YOU NEED ME TO SHOW YOU HOW TO GET FREE SUBWAY RIDES?

I HAD THE FEELING JUSTIN WASN'T THE KIND OF GUY TO EXAGGERATE MUCH.

FOUR NIGHTS IN BROWNSVILLE

Night One.

AND HE WAS RIGHT.

BROWNSVILLE LIVED UP TO HIS WORD.

FORGET TYRELL! HE'S ALREADY SHOT!

JUST SHUT UP AND RUN!

BLAM

Night Two.

WHAT DO YOU MEAN YOU DON'T HAVE A WALLET?

Night Three.

ACTUALLY, NIGHT THREE WAS FINE.

Night Four.

NIGHT FOUR'S WHEN THINGS GOT COMPLICATED.

NO!

HE'S ONLY A KID!

WANDA, C'MON! I'M JUST THINKING ABOUT HIS FUTURE!

NO, YOU'RE THINKING ABOUT WHAT MESSED UP WAYS YOU CAN EXPLOIT MY BOY!

HENRY'S GETTING OLDER. HE'S GONNA WANT MONEY.

AND I'VE GOT WORK. WORK THAT COULD SUPPORT YOU BOTH.

EVERYBODY WINS HERE.

YOU THINK WE NEED SUPPORT?!

I HAVEN'T RELIED ON ANYONE IN MY WHOLE DAMN LIFE!

I'M NOT ABOUT TO START WITH YOU!

JUST BACK THE HELL OFF, NOAH.

AND STAY AWAY FROM MY SON!

MY IMMEDIATE THOUGHT WAS TO NOT GET INVOLVED.

BUT I RECOGNIZED SOMETHING IN HER.

E-EXCUSE ME, UM, MA'AM?

IS EVERYTHING OKAY?

"MA'AM"?!

YOU'RE ONE AWFULLY WELL-MANNERED METH HEAD!

SOMETHING FROM MY OWN MOTHER.

YEAH, EVERYTHING'S BEEN "OKAY", ESPECIALLY BEFORE YOU STARTED TALKING TO ME!

NOW MAYBE DO ME A FAVOR AND SHUT YOUR PASTY-ASS MOUTH SO I CAN GET BACK TO "OKAY"!

THE SAME FIGHT.

THE SAME HEART.

RIGHT. SORRY.

HAVE A GOOD EVENING.

A REMINDER OF THE TIME BEFORE MY LIFE SPIRALED ALL TO HELL.

BEFORE ALL THIS:

I THINK OF GROWING UP IN GREECE.

NAFPLIO, MY HOME.

THERE WAS JUST THE TWO OF US.

WELL, AND EMIL. THE CLOSEST THING I EVER HAD TO A BROTHER.

IT WAS ACTUALLY PRETTY PLEASANT FOR A LONG TIME THERE.

THEN I FOUND OUT JUST HOW FAR ALONG MY DISEASE ALREADY WAS.

HOW MY BLOOD CELLS WERE DYING, WEAKENING MY IMMUNE SYSTEM AND BODY TO SUCH A POINT EVEN THE SMALLEST FALL COULD ALMOST END MY LIFE.

AND HOW
I BECAME A
DEAD VAMPIRE.

JOE KEATINGE
WRITER

RICHARD ELSON
ARTIST

ANTONIO FABELA
COLORIST

VC's CLAYTON COWLES
LETTERER

GABRIELE DELL'OTTO
COVER ARTIST

SKOTTIE YOUNG, ED MCGUINNESS & MARTE GRACIA
VARIANT COVER ARTISTS

DEDICATED TO ROY THOMAS AND GIL KANE, WHO STARTED IT ALL

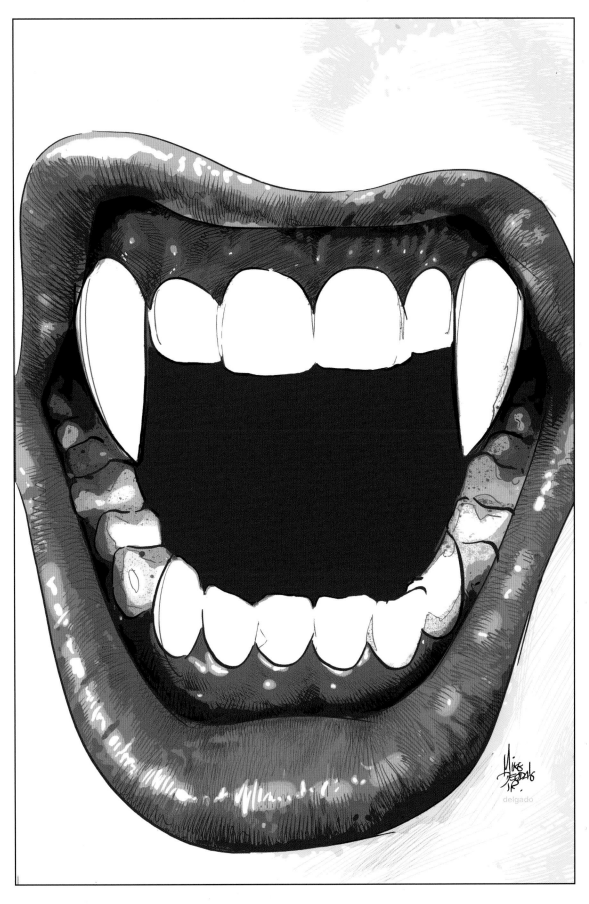

Morbius: The Living Vampire (2013) #2
Cover by **MIKE DEODATO JR.**

IT'S A DANGEROUS WORLD.

The Brownsville Apartment of Wanda & Henry Evans.

BROWNSVILLE, NEW YORK.

AND WHERE HAVE YOU BEEN, LITTLE MISTER?

IT ALWAYS HAS BEEN.

PEOPLE ACT LIKE THAT'S A NEW NOTION--THAT THERE WERE "GOOD OLD DAYS," BUT IT'S ALWAYS BEEN ROUGH.

IF ANYTHING, NOW IT'S MORE OBVIOUS. MORE OUT IN THE OPEN. MORE TRANSPARENT.

BASKETBALL, MOM. WITH CARL.

WELL, FIRST, SCHOOL. THEN BASKETBALL WITH CARL.

AND DID I TELL YOU YOU COULD PLAY BASKETBALL WITH CARL?

NO.

YOU'RE DAMN RIGHT I DIDN'T TELL YOU YOU COULD PLAY BASKETBALL WITH CARL.

YOU NEED TO COME HOME AFTER SCHOOL, HENRY.

RIGHT AWAY. EVERY DAY.

NO STOPPING.

BUT WHY?

WHY DO YOU THINK?

BELIEVE ME, IT'S A BAD, BAD WORLD.

THERE AIN'T ANY GOOD OUT THERE.

AND IT ALWAYS HAS BEEN.

THE DEATH OF MICHAEL MORBIUS.

YOU GET USED TO IT.

I'M BECKY; I'VE BEEN FOLLOWING YOU FOR A WHILE.

IS THAT CREEPY? I HOPE THAT'S NOT CREEPY.

YOU JUST DON'T SEE MANY PEOPLE STICKING UP FOR ANYONE IN BROWNSVILLE.

SO, YOU KNOW, YOU SEEMED LIKE A GOOD GUY TO MEET UP WITH.

ALTHOUGH, I'M SORRY WHEN WE MET...WELL, YOU GETTING KILLED...

I'LL BE FINE.

SO, WE'RE SKIPPING A HOSPITAL? MOST PEOPLE DON'T JUST GET UP AFTER GETTING SHOT IN THE CHEST.

I'M NOT MOST PEOPLE.

I'LL EXPLAIN LATER. I NEED TO LAY LOW RIGHT NOW.

WELL, COOL.

WHAT ARE YOUR THOUGHTS ON ABANDONED MOVIE THEATERS?

WHY SHOULD I BE SO SCARED?

OF THE GUY WHO BLASTED YOU FULL OF SHOTGUN?

MAYBE BECAUSE OF THE SHOTGUN PART?

LOOK, MAYBE GUYS LIKE HIM DON'T SCARE GUYS LIKE YOU, BUT THERE'S A HIERARCHY AROUND HERE AND SOMEHOW THIS WHITE DUDE WITH SPIKEY BLUE HAIR IS RIGHT ON TOP.

YOU THINK I FEEL SAFE WALKING ALONE-- AT ALL? AT ANY TIME?

WHY AREN'T YOU HOME?

UH, WHAT DO YOU THINK WE'RE DOING HERE?

THIS IS MY HOME.

YOU'RE--?

YEAH, DUDE; I'M HOMELESS TOO!

I DON'T SQUAT AROUND CONDEMNED THEATERS BECAUSE I'M BORED OF MY PARK AVENUE PENTHOUSE!

SCIENCE MAY HAVE MADE YOU A VAMPIRE, BUT IT SURE DIDN'T DO MUCH FOR YOUR PERCEPTION SKILLS.

THIS IS TRUE.

LOOK AT *THIS* GUY!

DIDN'T I KILL YOU AN HOUR AGO?

AND YOU TWO ARE BUDDIES?

THAT IS BEAUTIFUL.

I BELIEVE THE BOY'S MOTHER ASKED YOU TO LEAVE HIM ALONE.

I BELIEVE I DON'T GIVE A CRAP. LET THE BOY DECIDE FOR HIMSELF.

YOU COOL WITH ME, HENRY?

Y-YES...

THEN THERE YOU GO. HE'S MADE UP HIS MIND.

THIS ISN'T A DEBATE, NOAH!

WE'RE TAKING HIM HOME.

THE HELL YOU ARE.

ROCHELLE...?

UNH!

THANK YOU, GIRL.

AS FOR YOU, TOUGH GUY...YOU READY TO TURN AROUND?

GO HOME? RUN AWAY AGAIN?

SMOKE WHATEVER IT IS YOU SMOKE UNTIL YOU FORGET ABOUT ALL THIS?

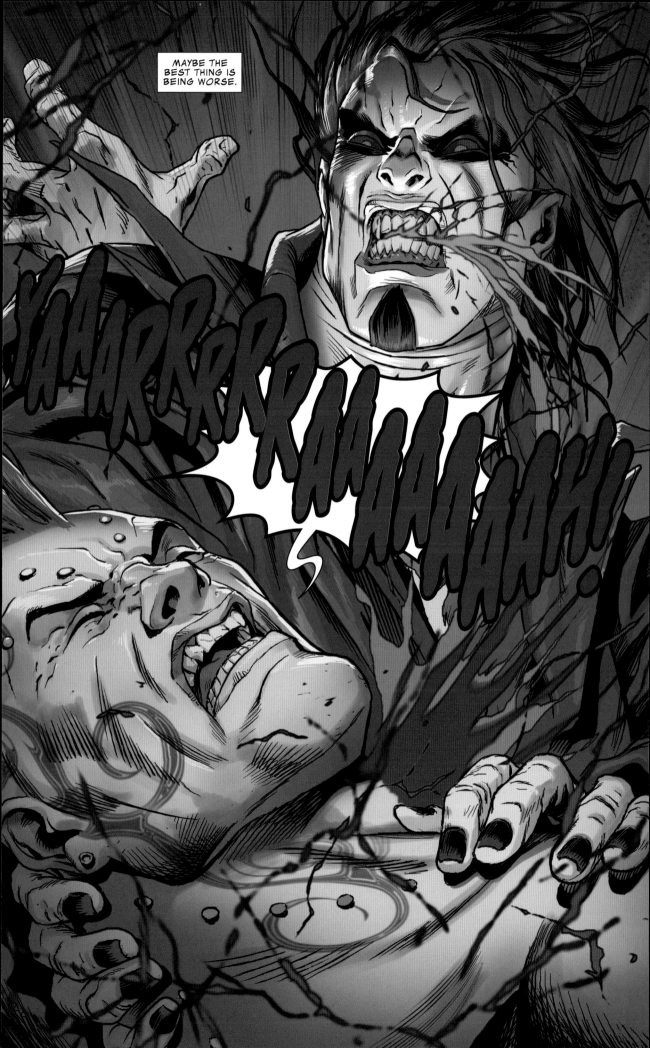

TO RIGHT A WRONG

Morbius: The Living Vampire (2013) #3
Cover by **DAVID LOPEZ**

I'M PRONE TO BAD IDEAS.

IT'S WHY I'M A VAMPIRE.

OOPS.

IT'S WHY I UNINTENTIONALLY KILLED MY BEST FRIEND AFTER BECOMING ONE.

IT'S WHY I ESCAPED FROM PRISON.

THUD

THIS IS WHY I'M IN BROWNSVILLE...

WELL--THIS IS EMBARRASSING.

...AND WHY EVERYONE HERE IS GOING TO DIE.

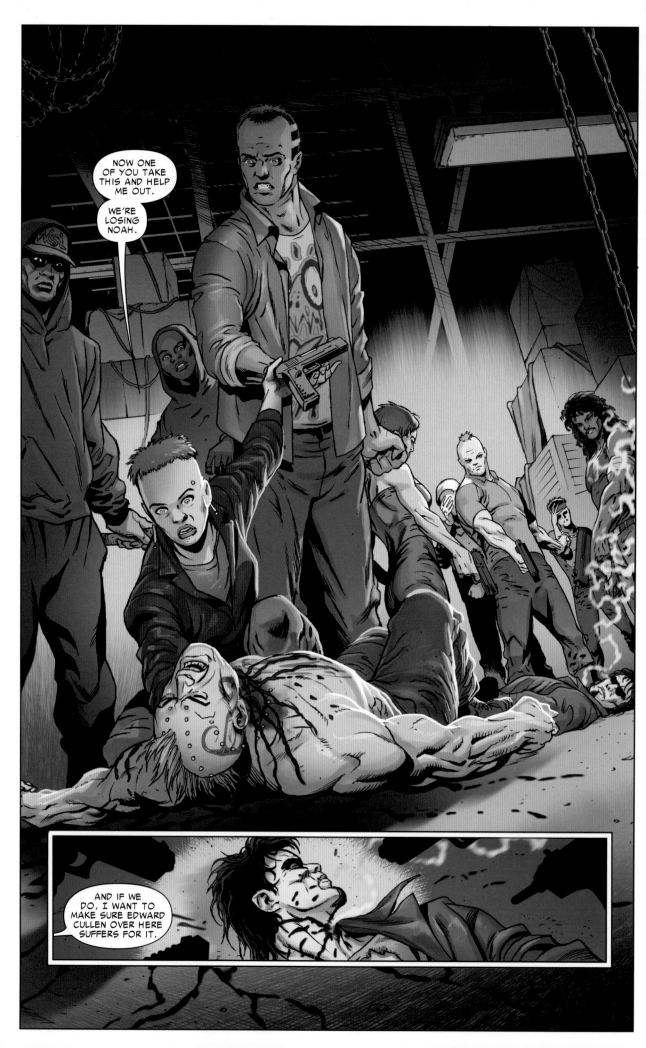

MORE BAD IDEAS.

FAIR ENOUGH.

WE PROBABLY SHOULDN'T HANG OUT WITH MY "FRIEND" EITHER.

AND WHY ARE YOU DRAWING HIM, ANYWAY? AREN'T ALL THOSE FOLKS SUPPOSED TO REPRESENT THE GOOD IN BROWNSVILLE?

I GOT THE WRONG IMPRESSION. HE STOOD UP TO NOAH, AFTER ALL.

I THOUGHT HE WAS A GOOD GUY.

I DON'T THINK HE IS.

YEAH. YOU'RE PROBABLY RIGHT. I WAS PROBABLY WRONG.

LET'S JUST HOPE THIS NEXT IDEA WORKS.

I'M OUT OF OPTIONS.

DOCTOR MICHAEL.

I GOTTA TELL YOU. MY ORIGINAL PLAN WAS TO TORTURE THE HELL OUT OF YOU AND YOUR FRIENDS.

I'M PRETTY VINDICTIVE WHEN IT COMES TO PEOPLE BITING MY LOVED ONES.

DESPITE HIS STUPID HAIR AND THOSE AWFUL PIERCINGS THERE'S A LOT ABOUT NOAH I LOVE.

EVERYONE THINKS HE'S SO BAD, SO CRUEL, BUT THE TRUTH IS HE'S THE ONLY ONE WHO DOES A DAMN THING FOR BROWNSVILLE.

SO YOU SAY YOU CAN HELP? WELL, THEN, THAT WORKS OUT JUST EVER SO WONDERFULLY FOR THE TWO OF US.

'CAUSE MY BOYS ARE OUT OF OPTIONS HERE.

I DON'T BUY FOR A MINUTE YOU'RE A DOCTOR, BUT FIXING UP MY MAN'S THE ONE CHANCE YOU'VE GOT.

HELP MY GUYS ALREADY WORKING ON NOAH SEW HIM BACK TOGETHER AND I WON'T DO ALL THE HORRIBLE THINGS I HAD PLANNED.

IF HE DIES?

THAT AIN'T GONNA WORK OUT TOO GREAT FOR YOU AND YOURS.

WHAT'S THE SITUATION?

THE SITUATION IS YOU TORE THIS GUY APART.

I'M DOING WHAT I CAN-- I STOPPED THE BLEEDING, BUT... I DON'T KNOW WHAT ELSE *CAN* BE DONE.

I THOUGHT YOU WERE A FIELD MEDIC?

MAN, *NO!* I WAS IN THE ARMY RESERVES, BUT NEVER EVEN SAW COMBAT.

LOST MY ARM IN A CAR ACCIDENT BEFORE I COULD.

AND YOUR MEDICAL TRAINING?

THEN YOU DON'T KNOW WHAT YOU'RE DOING.

I GOT A CERTIFICATE IN FIRST AID FROM THE COMMUNITY CENTER.

THEN WE'RE IN A WHOLE LOT OF TROUBLE.

WHAT I DO KNOW IS ROCHELLE THOUGHT I COULD DO SOMETHING HERE AND THREATENED ME IF I DIDN'T.

YOU THINK THERE'S ANYTHING WE CAN DO?

AT THIS POINT?

...MAYBE.

NO. NO, I ACTUALLY DON'T.

NOAH'S DEFINITELY DYING.

AND THERE'S NOTHING WE CAN DO.

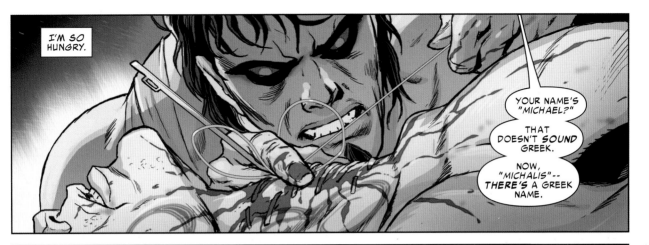

I'M SO HUNGRY.

YOUR NAME'S "MICHAEL?"

THAT DOESN'T *SOUND* GREEK.

NOW, "MICHALIS"-- *THERE'S* A GREEK NAME.

SO VERY HUNGRY.

THE STRESS IS JUST MAKING THE BLOOD LUST WORSE.

I KNEW A MICHALIS. GOOD GUY.

HOW COME YOU'RE NOT "MICHALIS?"

MY MOTHER PREFERRED "MICHAEL."

MAKING THE COUNTDOWN TO ME LOSING IT AGAIN GO BY EVEN FASTER.

IS NOAH ST. GERMAIN *REALLY* HIS NAME?

HA HA-- NAH, NOT AT ALL.

DUDE'S NAME IS DAVE BRILL. I DUNNO WHERE "NOAH" CAME FROM.

HE DISAPPEARED FOR A WHILE--AND WHEN HE CAME BACK, HE BUFFED UP, HAD THAT CRAZY HAIR, AND CHANGED HIS NAME.

WEIRDEST THING.

GAK!

VASQUEZ!

STAY DOWN!

WE'RE NOT CLOSE TO FINISHED HERE! YOU KEEP THIS UP AND YOUR WOUNDS WILL COME UNDONE!

AND SUDDENLY IT ALL GETS TO ME, THE BLOOD, THE HUNGER, THE ANGER...

I CAN'T TAKE IT ANY LONGER...

THE FIRST TIME WE MET, I WAS LAYING LOW.

HOLDING BACK, TRYING NOT TO GET NOTICED.

BUT RIGHT NOW? THERE ARE PEOPLE WHOSE LIVES ARE DEPENDING ON US NOT MESSING THIS UP RIGHT NOW.

SO, STAY DOWN!

THRAWK

BEHIND THE MASK

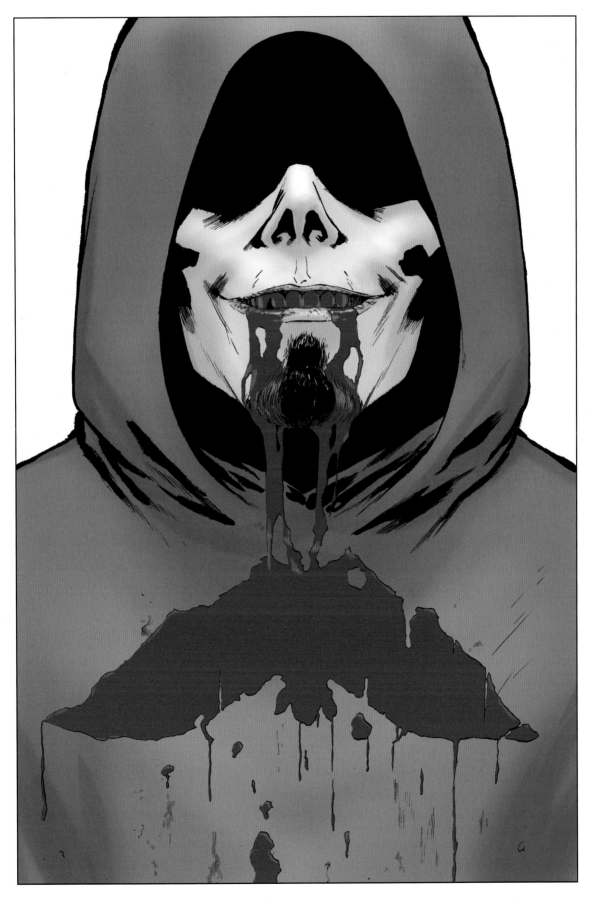

Morbius: The Living Vampire (2013) #4
Cover by **DAVID LOPEZ**

BROWNSVILLE. YEARS AGO.

I'M KIND OF A VAMPIRE.
KLITCH
AAARRRGGHH!
CARTER WILL BE FINE IF YOU HELP HIM RIGHT NOW.
I KNOW YOU HAVE MY FRIENDS--KEEP THEM SAFE AND CARTER LIVES.
WHY WOULD I TRUST YOU AFTER EVERYTHING YOU'VE DONE?
YOU'RE TOO LATE, ANYWAY. THEY'RE BEING TAKEN CARE OF.

ELI'S DINER.

BROWNSVILLE WAS KEPT IN LINE.

BUT HE'S GONE NOW.

THANKS TO YOU.

AND NOW... YOU'VE GOT NO IDEA WHAT KINDA FLOODGATES ARE OPENING.

"I DUNNO WHO JUST ROLLED IN HERE.

"BUT AS SOON AS WORD IS OUT THAT BROWNSVILLE IS VULNERABLE...

"THE VULTURES ARE GONNA FLY RIGHT IN.

"AND THEY AIN'T BEEN FED. NOT FOR A LONG, LONG TIME.

"THEY'RE GONNA WANNA TEAR NOAH'S CORPSE APART. TEAR UP THIS LITTLE EMPIRE OF HIS UNTIL THERE AIN'T ANYBODY LEFT ALIVE."

SO, YOU THINK YOU TOUGH? YOU THINK THAT EYEBALL FRIEND OF YOURS WAS A PAIN IN THE ASS?

HE WAS, YEAH.

WELL, I'LL TELL YOU NOW-- WHEN THE COMING STORM ROLLS THROUGH BROWNSVILLE? YOU'RE GONNA MISS YER FRIEND.

THEN, I PROMISE YOU...

...YOU'RE GONNA WISH YOU NEVER EVEN HEARD THE NAME "NOAH ST. GERMAIN."

WELL, *THAT'S* JUST SPLENDID NEWS.

CHONDRA REPORTS WE'VE GOT OUR NOAH BACK. WE ABSOLUTELY COULDN'T AFFORD HAVING ANYONE AUTOPSY OUR FINE IMPROVEMENTS ON OUR POOR BOY.

LOOSE ENDS ARE JUST *THE WORST.*

NORTH BROTHER ISLAND.

DON'T YOU AGREE, JUSTIN?

I...I GOT THE VAMPIRE TO BROWNSVILLE... JUST LIKE YOU WANTED...

YOU MOST CERTAINLY DID. AND AS PROMISED, I'LL EXPEDITE YOUR WIFE'S RETURN HOME.

I'M SURE SHE'LL BE *THRILLED*-- SHE DIDN'T SHOW EVEN THE SLIGHTEST HINT OF STOCKHOLM SYNDROME.

AS FOR MORBIUS, I WAS CERTAINLY RIGHT IN THINKING HE WAS THE ELEMENT BROWNSVILLE WAS MISSING.

I TRIED WITH NOAH--MADE HIM STRONGER, GAVE HIM A MORE...DRAMATIC LOOK, FUNDED HIS ENDEAVOR--BUT HE NEVER QUITE CAME TOGETHER.

BUT, MORBIUS-- A *"LIVING"* VAMPIRE.

SUCH AN ODD CONCEPT, YET SO MUCH POTENTIAL.

A WILDCARD AFTER MY OWN HEART.

VIVA LA REVOLUCION!

Morbius: The Living Vampire (2013) #5
Cover by **DAVID LOPEZ**

YOU'RE GONNA DAMN WELL HAVE TO BE!

YOU'RE PART OF BROWNSVILLE NOW!

THAT MEANS YOU DO WHAT WE ALL DO--

YOU MAKE GOOD WITH WHAT YOU HAVE AND, YEAH, REALIZE CHANCES ARE NOT IN YOUR FAVOR-- AND DO BETTER ANYWAY.

BECKY, I DON'T THINK--

LOOK, YEAH. MAYBE ON YOUR OWN THINGS WOULD JUST GET WORSE. MAYBE STANDING UP ON YOUR OWN ONLY LEADS TO MORE DISASTER.

I DON'T KNOW.

BUT I DO KNOW YOU'RE NOT ON YOUR OWN.

YOU'RE PART OF A WHOLE NEIGHBORHOOD NOW.

A NEIGHBORHOOD THAT CAN STAND UP TOGETHER...

I WANT TO MAKE SOMETHING CLEAR. ABOUT WHAT JUST HAPPENED HERE.

I DIDN'T HELP ANYONE. IT'S NOT MY NATURE.

I JUST HURT A LOT OF PEOPLE. IT'S WHAT I DO.

THE FEW OF YOU WHO KNEW ME BEFORE TODAY--WELL, YOU KNEW ME. YOU'VE SEEN WHAT I AM.

SEEN WHAT HARM I DO.

YOU'VE SEEN I'M NOT A GOOD PERSON. I TRY, BUT-- THAT'S JUST NOT HOW IT WORKS.

I COULDN'T HAVE DONE THIS WITHOUT YOU. IF I DIDN'T HAVE YOU TO FIX THIS MESS I MADE--TO REPAIR THE PEOPLE I HURT--IT WOULD JUST GET WORSE. RELENTLESSLY WORSE.

BUT, YOU DID. YOU'RE HERE.

YOU'RE THE ONES SHOWING THOSE WHO WOULD OPPRESS YOU THAT THEIR LIVES ARE IN YOUR HANDS. THAT THEIR FATES ARE YOURS TO DECIDE.

THEY'LL KNOW THE PEOPLE OF BROWNSVILLE ARE STRONG. THAT THEY DON'T CAVE INTO THE FEAR OF GREEDY MEN AND WOMEN WHO WOULD OTHERWISE PROFIT OFF THEIR MISERY.

BUT IT SHOULD BE CLEAR, YOUR SALVATION IS YOUR OWN.

BLAM

I'LL CHECK IT OUT; STAY HERE.

I'M SURE IT'S NOTHING I CAN'T HANDLE.

WAS THAT A GUN? I THOUGHT EVERYBODY WAS DOWN.

THEY WERE.

Y'KNOW, MAYBE WE SHOULD CELEBRATE YOUR FAT HEAD'S APPEARANCE ON THE WALL BY PAINTING THE INSIDES TOO.

MAYBE WE SHOULD. THE THEATER'S GROWN ON ME.

IT BETTER HAVE. YOU'RE STUCK AROUND HERE NOW, DUDE.

PRETTY SURE THIS MEANS YOU'RE LIFETIME PRESIDENT OF THE NEIGHBORHOOD WATCH.

THIS MIGHT NOT BE A GOOD THING.

I HAVE A LOT OF ENEMIES. THE AUTHORITIES ALONE WON'T BE HAPPY ONCE WORD GETS AROUND.

YEAH, WELL; YOUR HIDING OUT DAYS ARE OVER ANYWAY, MAN.

GIANT PAINTED FACE OR NO GIANT PAINTED FACE--PEOPLE ALL OVER ARE GONNA KNOW ABOUT LAST NIGHT IF THEY DON'T ALREADY.

I HOPE THAT'S FOR THE BETTER.

IT ALREADY IS, MIKE.

EVERYTHING IS DIFFERENT NOW.

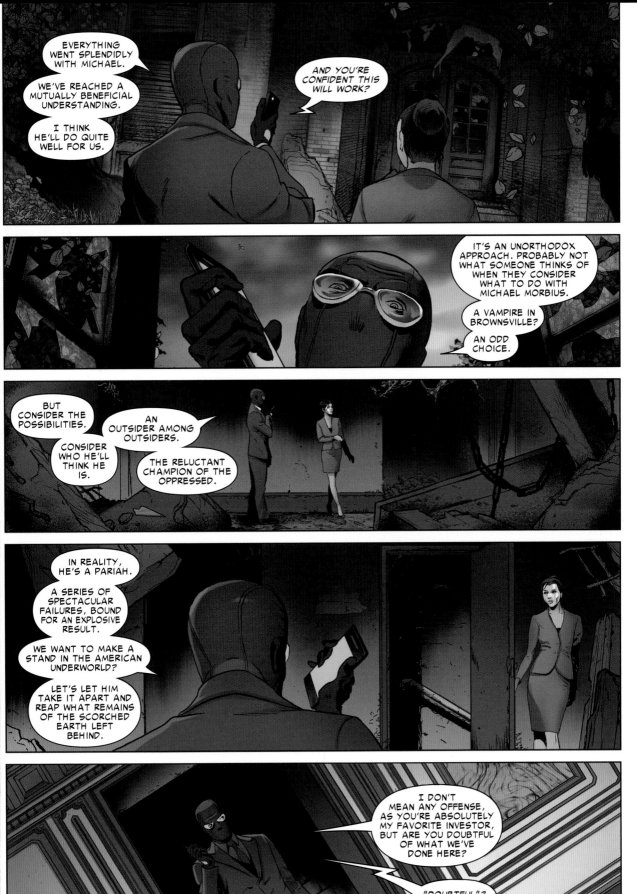

EVERYTHING WENT SPLENDIDLY WITH MICHAEL.

WE'VE REACHED A MUTUALLY BENEFICIAL UNDERSTANDING.

I THINK HE'LL DO QUITE WELL FOR US.

AND YOU'RE CONFIDENT THIS WILL WORK?

IT'S AN UNORTHODOX APPROACH. PROBABLY NOT WHAT SOMEONE THINKS OF WHEN THEY CONSIDER WHAT TO DO WITH MICHAEL MORBIUS.

A VAMPIRE IN BROWNSVILLE?

AN ODD CHOICE.

BUT CONSIDER THE POSSIBILITIES.

AN OUTSIDER AMONG OUTSIDERS.

CONSIDER WHO HE'LL THINK HE IS.

THE RELUCTANT CHAMPION OF THE OPPRESSED.

IN REALITY, HE'S A PARIAH.

A SERIES OF SPECTACULAR FAILURES, BOUND FOR AN EXPLOSIVE RESULT.

WE WANT TO MAKE A STAND IN THE AMERICAN UNDERWORLD?

LET'S LET HIM TAKE IT APART AND REAP WHAT REMAINS OF THE SCORCHED EARTH LEFT BEHIND.

I DON'T MEAN ANY OFFENSE, AS YOU'RE ABSOLUTELY MY FAVORITE INVESTOR, BUT ARE YOU DOUBTFUL OF WHAT WE'VE DONE HERE?

"DOUBTFUL"? OF MICHAEL?

OF COURSE NOT.

Morbius: The Living Vampire (2013) #6
Cover by **DAVID LOPEZ**

Horizon Labs, New York City.

LAST NIGHT. AFTER HOURS.

THIS IS WHAT PASSES FOR A CUTTING EDGE SCIENTIFIC BRAIN TRUST THESE DAYS?

REALLY?

EVERYTHING LOOKS SO... DATED.

IT WOULD HAVE A CERTAIN NAIVE CHARM IF IT WASN'T SO PATHETICALLY, WELL, OLD.

WHAT THE HELL?

EXCUSE ME, MA'AM--YOU SHOULDN'T BE HERE.

I NEED TO ASK YOU TO LEAVE.

HM. ARE YOU?

I'VE GOT ANOTHER IDEA.

KRIZZIRAT

LET'S *CURE* THE WORLD OF YOU.

Brownsville,
New York.
THE MORNING AFTER.

MIKE, C'MON-- DON'T BE SUCH A WHINER!

IT'S GONNA HELP OUT!

NO, BECKY...

...I CAN FIGHT MORE EFFECTIVELY WITHOUT THE HEADSET.

IT'S TOO CUMBERSOME.

THRAMM

VERY WELL.

FOOM

IT'S A VISUAL NEURAL DEHABILITATOR, SPECIFIED TO YOUR *SPECIAL* GENETIC MAKEUP.

IN LAYMAN'S TERMS, I TOOK ADVANTAGE OF YOUR DISTASTE FOR *BRIGHT* LIGHTS.

I CAME PREPARED, MICHAEL; I'VE LEARNED FROM MY PAST MISTAKES.

THWIP

HOPEFULLY, YOU'LL DO THE SAME.

MICHAEL?

CAN YOU HEAR ME?

M-MAX MODELL...?

YES, MICHAEL.

IT'S ME, OLD FRIEND. WELCOME BACK TO THE LAND OF THE LIVING.

AND WELCOME BACK TO HORIZON LABS.

I APOLOGIZE FOR THE MEANS.

WOULD YOU CARE FOR A DRINK?

UM. I SUPPOSE I AM A BIT PARCHED.

I'M ASSUMING YOU'D ENJOY SOME BLOOD?

HUMAN, IF YOU HAVE IT.

THAT CAN BE ACCOMMODATED.

THANK YOU, BUT...

...JUST WHAT EXACTLY'S GOING ON HERE?

WHY WOULD SPIDER-MAN BRING ME TO HORIZON?

THIS IS A **LOT**.

I MAY BE HERE A WHILE.

CONSIDER IT A TESTAMENT TO YOUR TIRELESS PURSUIT OF CREATING A CURE TO ASSIST THE GREATER GOOD.

EXCEPT FOR WHEN HE EXHUMED THE DEAD CONNORS BOY.*

...RIGHT.

*BACK WHEN HE WAS TRYING TO FIND A CURE IN AMAZING SPIDER-MAN #689! --SANA, THE MORE-OR-LESS LIVING HUMAN

I CAN'T SAY I APPRECIATE THE EXTRA SPIDER-BOTS. THEY'RE DISTURBING THE CRIME SCENE.

THEY'RE EQUIPPED TO PROPERLY ANALYZE THE CRIME SCENE AND PROCESS THE DATA IN WAYS YOU FOOLS COULD NEVER HOPE TO.

YES, WELL--

DO YOU REALLY NEED THIS MANY? SEVEN SEEMS EXCESSIVE.

ODD.

I ONLY CALLED IN THREE.

KRAKA-THROOM

OH, DEAR!

LOOKS LIKE SOMEONE ELSE CALLED IN THEM ALL.

PERHAPS YOU SHOULD CALL OFF YOUR--UM, SPIDER-MAN?

M-MY SPIDER-SENSE... FEELS LIKE IT'S ON FIRE...

...OVERLOADED...

WELL, ON THE PLUS SIDE...

...I CAN'T SAY I DON'T APPRECIATE THE OPPORTUNITY TO DESTROY ANYTHING CREATED BY YOU.

WHAT DO YOU WANT?

HE DID HAVE THE IDEA ABOUT ME COMING BACK HERE, TO SHOW YOU JUST HOW MUCH WE CAN BREAK YOU WITHOUT A THOUGHT.

KRAK

TO SHOW YOU HOW FUTILE PURSUING US WOULD BE.

MY POINT'S THIS: YOU GUYS WILL HAVE NO IDEA WHAT'S COMING.

P-PLEASE... WHATEVER YOU NEED... JUST DON'T HURT ANYONE ELSE HERE...I'LL DO WHATEVER YOU WANT...

MAX, NO!

THE ALWAYS RASH...ALWAYS *STUPID* MICHAEL MORBIUS.

YOU'RE GOING TO EMBARRASS YOURSELF, OLD MAN.

YOU DON'T THINK I'M READY FOR YOU?

YOU DON'T THINK I DIDN'T RESEARCH EVERYTHING THERE IS TO KNOW ABOUT YOU? YOUR EVERY WEAKNESS?

THRAGG

I COULD END YOU IN THE BLINK OF AN EYE.

IT WOULD BE NOTHING TO ME.

THROOM

BUT SCREWING WITH YOU IS SO MUCH MORE SATISFYING.

AND THANKFULLY, IT PAYS THE BILLS.

YOU KNOW, I THOUGHT YOU'D APPRECIATE BEATING UP SPIDER-MAN.

I WAS MORE IMPRESSED BY MAX MODELL.

WE SEEM LIKE KINDRED SPIRITS, YOU AND I.

I WOULDN'T GO THAT FAR, MR. ROSE.

I DON'T TRUST *ANYONE* OLDER THAN TWENTY-FIVE.

VERY WELL.

DID YOU GET WHAT I REQUIRED?

Funds transfer COMPLETE

OK

I JUST NEED TO HIT UP A.I.M. AND WE'LL HAVE EVERY COMPONENT WE NEED TO BUILD THIS THING.

AND YOU'RE POSITIVE IT'LL HAVE THE RESULT I DESIRE?

YOU ASKED FOR SOMETHING EXPLOSIVE.

AND I MEAN, REALLY? EXPLODING'S ONE THING...

Morbius: The Living Vampire (2013) #7
Cover by **DAVID LOPEZ**

AAARAAAAGGHH!

KRIZZIRAT

I'M ASKING YOU ONCE MORE, TELL ME WHERE--

DOWN THE HALL, THIRD DOOR ON THE LEFT.

THERE YOU GO.

YOUR HELP IS APPRECIATED.

YAAARGH!

SKIZZIRAT

I'LL ALWAYS REMEMBER YOUR GENEROSITY.

HERE WE GO-- A HYPER-COMPRESSED NEGATIVE ZONE COSMIC RAY.

I DIDN'T EVEN KNOW THAT'S A THING.

ROSE, IT'S HARROW.

THE POWER SOURCE IS SECURED.

TELEPORT ME OUT.

GLADLY.

THRA-THROOM

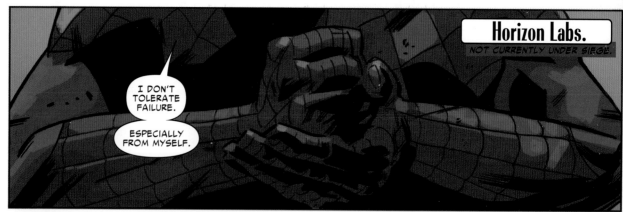

I DON'T TOLERATE FAILURE.

ESPECIALLY FROM MYSELF.

WHAT HAPPENED WITH NIKOLETA HARROW WAS INTOLERABLE.

WE WERE FOOLISHLY CAUGHT OFF GUARD, BEATEN DOWN LIKE AMATEURS.

HER INTENTION WAS TO BELITTLE US, BUT IN THAT SHE FAILED. I LEARNED EVERYTHING I REQUIRED TO DESTROY HER.

NOW WE'RE PREPARED.

WE KNOW WHAT HARROW KNOWS ABOUT US.

AND, IN TURN, WE KNOW HOW TO COUNTER HER EVERY MOVE.

WE WILL FIND HER. WE WILL STOP HER. WE WILL SHOW HER THE HUMILITY SHE ATTEMPTED TO BRING UPON US.

BUT WHO WE WERE BEFORE WAS NOT ENOUGH.

WE WILL BECOME...

...SUPERIOR.

I CAN GET BEHIND "SUPERIOR," SPIDER-MAN.

THIS NEW SUIT CERTAINLY BEATS THE HOODIE.

AND YOU'RE SURE *THIS* IS WHAT YOU WANT?

AS LONG AS MY EXACT SPECIFICATIONS WERE MET, ABSOLUTELY.

THEY'RE MET.

VERY WELL, MODELL...

BEHOLD THE DOWNFALL OF NIKOLETA HARROW!

UM...

...HUH.

DID YOU MENTION--

OH, HEAVENS NO. I'M NOT THAT BRAVE.

WHAT NOW?!

WELL, THE "DOWNFALL," THE DEVICE...ARE YOU SURE YOU DON'T WANT TO TRY TO MINIATURIZE IT?

DON'T YOU THINK I WOULD HAVE IF THAT WAS AN OPTION?!

MAYBE IT IS AND YOU'RE JUST NOT SEEING IT.

I SENSE YOUR EGO'S BEEN A BIT BRUISED. YOU'RE UPSET.

POSSIBLY NOT THINKING CLEARLY.

HOW DARE YOU QUESTION--

COME ON, STOP IT.

I'M HELPING YOU OUT.

NOW, LOOK. LET ME BORROW THE DEVICE FOR A SECOND.

THE IDEA'S TO BLOCK HER CONTROL OVER YOUR SPIDER-SENSE, CORRECT?

SO, YOU'RE GOING WITH THE HYPOTHESIS SHE'S TIED INTO YOUR SENSES--TO PUT IT SIMPLY-- *"FREQUENCY?"* AND YOU'RE SHUTTING OUT HER CONTROL BY REROUTING THE SIGNAL?

PRECISELY.

THEN WE DON'T NEED NINETY PERCENT OF THIS.

WHY GO OUT OF YOUR WAY TO REROUTE HER SIGNAL?

JUST--GIVE ME A SECOND. I CAN HANDLE THIS.

IT'S CERTAINLY NICE TO HAVE ANOTHER SUPER-SCIENTIST AROUND.

WE'LL SEE.

TRY THIS ON. SHOULD SLIP IN RIGHT UNDER YOUR MASK.

HOW COULD THIS POSSIBLY BE ENOUGH TO--

IT'S NOT DOING WHAT YOU WANTED IT TO.

INSTEAD OF WORRYING ABOUT HER SIGNAL, IT JUST SHUTS OFF YOUR SPIDER-SENSE. WHICH, SURE, IS A DOWNSIDE.

BUT, WELL--

YOU'LL HAVE *ME.*

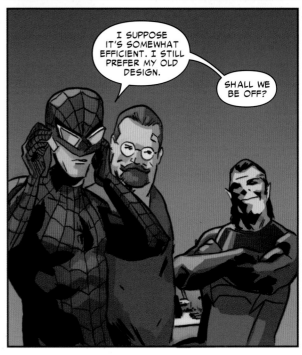

I SUPPOSE IT'S SOMEWHAT EFFICIENT. I STILL PREFER MY OLD DESIGN.

SHALL WE BE OFF?

North Brother Island.
A BIT LATER.

HOW'S EVERYTHING COMING ALONG?

JUST ABOUT DONE.

I WON'T BRING THIS UP AGAIN, BUT I'M A LITTLE CONFUSED HERE.

AN "ULTIMATE NULLIFIER" JUST SEEMS SO--I DUNNO--PASSÉ?

I FEEL LIKE EVERYONE HAS ONE THESE DAYS.

I COULD CERTAINLY MAKE YOU SOMETHING MORE...MODERN?

I'M A SUCKER FOR NOSTALGIA.

HOW MUCH LONGER WILL IT BE?

ONLY A MINUTE.

YOUR BOOTLEG ULTIMATE NULLIFIER'S MORE OR LESS READY TO GO.

NOT A FRACTION AS POWERFUL AS AN ACTUAL NULLIFIER, BUT AS POWERFUL AS WE AGREED TO.

YOU'LL BE GOOD TO ANNIHILATE THOUSANDS OF LIVES IN THE BLINK OF AN EYE.

EXCELLENT.

I TAKE IT YOU'RE PREPARED TO DEAL WITH MORBIUS AND--

ALREADY IN MOTION.

BY MY GUESS, THEY'LL BE WHERE I'VE LED THEM TO WITHIN THE NEXT HOUR OR SO, MAYBE LESS. A SIMPLETON SHOULD BE ABLE TO TRACK THE SIGNAL USING THE SPIDER-BOTS.

YOU'RE AWFULLY CASUAL ABOUT ALL THIS.

WHAT'S THERE TO WORRY ABOUT?

THEY'LL COME. WE'LL FIGHT. WHAT HAPPENS WILL HAPPEN.

I'LL GET THEM TO WHERE THEY NEED TO BE.

ALSO ALREADY IN MOTION.

JUST BE SURE TO HOLD UP YOUR END OF THE BARGAIN.

THEN I SHOULD BE GOING.

IT'S BEEN A PLEASURE DOING BUSINESS WITH YOU.

CEASE YOUR COMPLAINING AND HOLD ON!

IT'S LOOKING LIKE IT. JUST FOLLOW THE HIGH LINE.

WHATEVER SHE WAS USING TO CONTROL THE SPIDER-BOTS IS RIGHT AT THE END, JUST WEST OF WASHINGTON SQUARE PARK.

VERY WELL. HANG TIGHT.

THOOM

UNH...

YOU HAD US AT A DISADVANTAGE BEFORE.

BUT YOU'RE BARELY MORE THAN A CHILD.

OVERLY CONFIDENT WITH AN INFLATED, UNDESERVED EGO.

YOU'LL BE YOUR OWN DOWNFALL.

KRATOOM

YOU'RE ONE TO TALK. I HEAR YOUR EGO'S WORSE THAN EVER.

PERHAPS.

BUT MINE'S EARNED.

KATAK

THRAAM

I WOULDN'T BE SO SURE.

FABAAM

FRANKLY, I THINK EVERYBODY HERE COULD DO WITH A LITTLE LESS PATTING THEMSELVES ON THE BACK.

OH, MORBIUS; YOU'RE EVER A SAD SACK.

BUT I SUPPOSE THAT'S PART OF YOUR APPEAL.

I'M NOT SURE I HAVE MUCH "APPEAL."

SURE YOU DO.

YOU'RE THE PERFECT PATSY.

MORBIUS!

THRA-THROOM

MICHAEL.

I--DOESN'T MATTER.

WHATEVER SHE USED TO CONTROL THE SPIDER-BOTS ONLY LEADS HERE. THERE'S NO SIGNAL TO GO ON.

MODELL, IT'S SPIDER-MAN.

I'VE LOST DR. MORBIUS.

OH, NO... NOT WHEN WE WERE SO CLOSE...

AND I'VE MADE SUCH PROGRESS ON HIS SERUM.

WITH HIS HELP, I THINK A CURE WOULD BE IN SIGHT.

FOR WHAT?

THERE'S NO USE WORRYING ABOUT IT NOW. I'M SENDING YOU AN ADDRESS.

YOU'LL WANT TO SEE THIS FOR YOURSELF. HORIZON HAS SOME CATALOGING TO DO.

THRA-THROOM

MORBIUS AND NIKOLETA HAVE ARRIVED, SIR.

NIKOLETA'S CERTAINLY PUNCTUAL, ISN'T SHE?

ARE YOU SURE YOU WOULDN'T RATHER SOMEONE ELSE DO THIS, SIR?

IT'S NOT LIKE YOU TO TAKE DIRECT ACTION.

ARE YOU KIDDING? I WOULDN'T MISS THIS FOR THE WORLD.

BROWNSVILLE'S MY PET PROJECT.

AND BESIDES, I SPENT A LOT OF OTHER PEOPLE'S MONEY ON THIS NULLIFIER.

IF ANYONE GETS TO PULL THE TRIGGER, IT'S ME.

CONSIDER THIS AN INDULGENCE.

KLIK

HERE IT COMES.

HERE WHAT COMES?!

Morbius: The Living Vampire (2013) #8
Cover by **DAVID LOPEZ**

I SUPPOSE IT'S OBVIOUS NOW--I NEVER HAD CONTROL TO BEGIN WITH.

I DO HAVE TO SAY-- NIKOLETA HAS DONE ME PROUD.

IMPRESSIVE POWER FOR A BOOTLEG.

MY DESTINY WAS NEVER MY OWN.

EVERYTHING I'VE EXPERIENCED HAS BEEN DETERMINED BY OTHERS.

SHALL WE GO HOME NOW, SIR?

NO, NO.

IT'S NO LONGER TIME TO HIDE IN THE SHADOWS.

THE TRIGGER'S BEEN PULLED; IT'S TIME TO FACE THE END.

HOWEVER, DO CALL MAKARIOA.

CONFIRM HIS ARRIVAL TIME.

IT DOES MAKE ME WONDER...

"WHEN WE'RE DONE HERE, THIS EARTH HERE WILL BE PROPERLY SCORCHED FOR OUR SHARED PURPOSE.

"WE CAN FINALLY BUILD A PROPER EMPIRE."

...WHAT IF I HAD MY OWN WAY?

WHERE WOULD I BE NOW?

SKRAAAAAAKKA-
THOOM
IT'S POWER.
THIS HAS ONLY EVER BEEN ABOUT POWER.
YOU REALLY THINK I'D LET MYSELF BE A BEACON FOR A LEVEL 1 ULTIMATE NULLIFIER IF I DIDN'T THINK I COULD SURVIVE?
THRAMM
YOU'RE A DENSE ONE, MICHAEL MORBIUS.

I THINK THIS WILL WORK, WANDA.

YOU BELIEVE HIM, BECKY?

YOU HAVE A BETTER IDEA?

SOME CRAZY DUDE IS TRYING TO BLOW UP BROWNSVILLE AND PIN IT ON MIKE.

MICHAEL.

SEEMS LIKE THE BEST WAY TO GO ABOUT IT.

I CAN'T PROMISE YOU THIS WILL WORK.

BUT I CAN PROMISE YOU I'M SURE AS HELL GOING TO TRY.

TIMES CERTAINLY HAVE CHANGED, MICHAEL.

I DIDN'T THINK MUCH OF YOU WHEN YOU FIRST SHOWED UP.

BUT THERE'S NO DENYING YOU'VE DONE A LOT OF GOOD.

WE'LL PLAY OUR PART HERE...

...YOU PLAY YOURS.

I AIM TO.

I HAVE BIG PLANS.

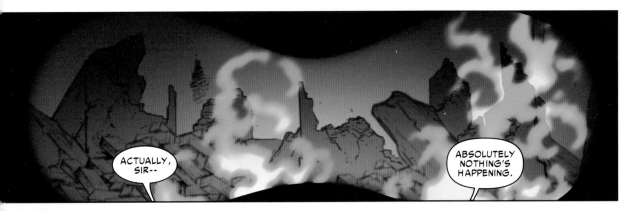

ACTUALLY, SIR--

ABSOLUTELY NOTHING'S HAPPENING.

I DON'T UNDERSTAND.

CHAOS ISN'T REIGNING?

WHY ISN'T CHAOS REIGNING?!

BROWNSVILLE APPEARS *EMPTY*, SIR.

EMPTY?!

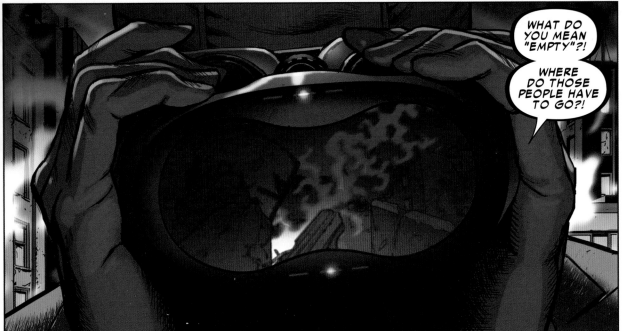

WHAT DO YOU MEAN "EMPTY"?!

WHERE DO THOSE PEOPLE HAVE TO GO?!

Y'KNOW, I HONESTLY DON'T GET WHY HE DIDN'T CALL US IN THE FIRST PLACE.

KIND OF THE POINT OF HAVING A MONSTER HAVEN IS TO, WELL, BE A HAVEN FOR MONSTERS.

WE WOULD'VE BEEN HAPPY TO HAVE HIM.

The Underground Passage to Monstropolis.
PREVIOUS HOME OF MICHAEL MORBIUS.

MIKE THINKS EVERYBODY HATES HIM.

HE'S GOT AN IMPRESSIVE MARTYR COMPLEX.

IS MORBIUS GOING BY "MIKE" NOW?

THIS IS TOTALLY THE COOLEST!

ARE YOU A DRACULA TOO?!

UM. NO. DRACULA ISN'T A--

‡SIGH‡ NEVERMIND, SURE, I'M A "DRACULA."

LEAVE THE MONSTERS ALONE, HENRY.

I'M SORRY, IS "MONSTERS" THE PROPER TERM? I DON'T WANT TO OFFEND ANYBODY.

OH, YEAH. WE'RE FINE WITH "MONSTERS."

LISTEN, YOU'RE ALL WELCOME TO STAY HERE UNTIL THINGS CALM DOWN, BUT ARE YOU SURE MICHAEL DIDN'T WANT ANY HELP UP ABOVE?

HE WAS INSISTENT HE HANDLE *THAT* PART ALONE.

WHATEVER'S HAPPENING...WELL, IT'S GOTTEN *REAL* PERSONAL.

THRAKKA THRAKKA THRAKKA

HELLO THERE, MICHAEL!

YOU RANG?

I DID. YOU'RE EVER SO BRAVE.

I CERTAINLY DIDN'T SEE *THAT* COMING.

IT'S NOT YOUR NATURE.

AND YOU BROUGHT A HELICOPTER. *THAT'S* BRAVE.

THIS SHOULD JUST BE *US*.

POINT TAKEN.

GO HOME, CHONDRA.

I'LL CALL NORTH BROTHER WHEN I'M DONE HERE.

THEN AGAIN, I DON'T IMAGINE THIS WILL TAKE LONG. WILL IT, MICHAEL?

Morbius: The Living Vampire (2013) #9
Cover by **MARCO CHECCHETTO**

ONE YEAR LATER

THE LIVING
PORTRAITS OF BROWNSVILLE
FROM ARTIST
BECKY BARNES

OPENING RECEPTION: 4·19 - 8 PM
GALERIE LANZ NY

BECKY BARNES-- IS THAT YOU?!

KIND OF!

I LOOK RIDICULOUS, RIGHT?!

YOU LOOK GOOD.

DAMN RIGHT SHE "LOOKS GOOD"!

LOOKS LIKE GETTING THE HECK OUTTA BROWNSVILLE IS DOING WONDERS FOR YOU.

IT'S ALL RIGHT, I GUESS.

SEEMS LIKE EVERYBODY'S EVEN MORE BROKE IN MANHATTAN.

WE'RE ALL STILL PRETTY BROKE BACK HOME, GIRL. NOTHING'S CHANGED THERE.

WHERE'S THE ONE OF ME?

HENRY! DON'T BE VAIN!

HA! IT'S FAIR--WE PUT HIM ALL OVER THE FLIER.

THIS WAY, SQUIRT.

LOOKS LIKE YOU'VE OFFICIALLY KICKED OFF MY BOY'S FIFTEEN MINUTES OF FAME.

HENRY DESERVES A LOT MORE. HE'S A REAL GOOD KID.

BEEN THROUGH SO MUCH.

WE ALL DID, DARLIN'. IT SEEMS TO BE WORKING OUT, THOUGH. YOU WITH YOUR BIG TIME NEW YORK ART SHOW AND ALL.

ABOUT TIME, THOUGH, RIGHT? STILL, WHATEVER. A FRIEND OF A FRIEND OWNS THIS PLACE.

THIS SHOW'S A FAVOR.

BUT, YEAH, I SUPPOSE IT IS WORKING OUT FOR US. ABOUT TIME, TOO.

EVERYTHING WAS NOT "WORKING OUT" FOR LONGER THAN I CAN REMEMBER.

BACK BEFORE--

WELL, YOU KNOW.

MICHAEL.

STILL NEVER HEARD FROM HIM, DID YOU?

...WANDA. YOU KNOW HE--

YOU NEVER KNOW, DEAR.

NO.

I'M PRETTY SURE I DO KNOW.

AFTER ALL...

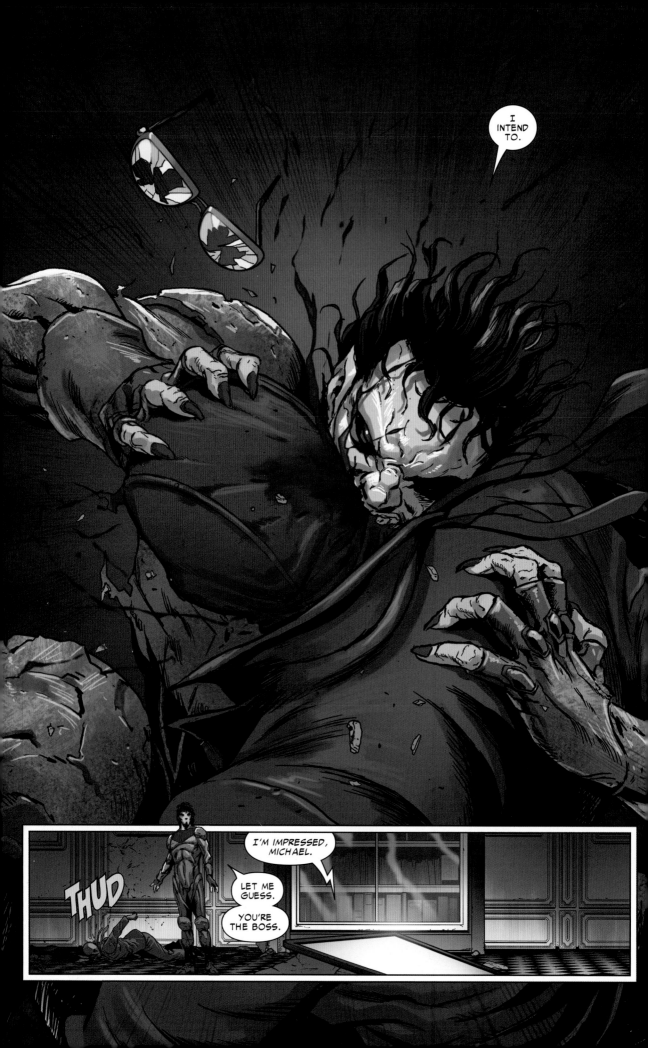

THEN ALL THINGS CONSIDERED, DOCTOR MORBIUS... ...WHAT DO YOU PLAN TO DO NOW?

"SO, WE'RE DONE HERE?"

LOOKING LIKE THAT'S A WRAP, BECKY!

NOT BAD FOR YOUR FIRST GALLERY OPENING, HUH?

IF YOU'RE HAPPY, I'M HAPPY.

THANKS FOR LETTING ME USE YOUR SPACE, MS. LANZ.

YOU NEED ANYTHING ELSE FROM ME FOR NOW? I PROMISED A FRIEND I'D GET A POST-SHOW DRINK.

NO, YOU'RE GOOD. I'LL SEE YOU WHEN I SEE YOU.

ENJOY YOUR NIGHT.

EVERYTHING WENT WELL?

SURE DID! NO THANKS TO YOU!

WOULD HAVE BEEN NICE IF YOU ACTUALLY SHOWED UP!

YOU KNOW I WOULD'VE IF I COULD'VE.

YEAH, YEAH. WHATEVER. I GET IT. JUST TIRED OF KEEPING YOU A SECRET.

THEY'LL KNOW ABOUT ME WHEN THE TIME'S RIGHT.

WELL, GREAT, SO FOR TODAY, YOU'RE STILL A SECRET. WHAT'S THAT MEAN FOR TOMORROW?

WHO KNOWS? I'M ENJOYING OUR CURRENT PLAN.

THE ONE THING I'VE LIKED MORE THAN ANYTHING ELSE I'VE TRIED.

Morbius: The Living Vampire (2013) #1
Variant cover by **ED McGUINNESS**

Morbius: The Living Vampire (2013) #1
Variant cover by **SKOTTIE YOUNG**

Morbius: The Living Vampire (2013) #2
Variant cover by **MARCOS MARTIN**

Morbius: The Living Vampire (2013) #3
Variant cover by **TOMM COKER**

Morbius: The Living Vampire (2013) #6
Variant cover by **PATRICK ZIRCHER**

FANG MAIL

And that's that.

Thank you for joining Rich Elson, Valentine De Landro and me for this unfortunately all-too-brief look into what happens when you put Morbius into a hoodie. This take wasn't my first pick as to what do with everyone's favourite science-based vampire, but it turned out to be a lot of fun in large part due to collaborating with Rich, Valentine and our highly valued pinch hitter fill-in artists. Our take was polarising to say the least, but the chance to get to do something so drastically different than status quo with a character is a rare opportunity and I'm overall happy with the results. Marvel was absolutely wonderful in launching and supporting this thing, so big thanks to those instrumental folks – Axel Alonso, C.B. Cebulski, Ryan Penagos, Arune Singh, James Viscardi, Ben Morse and Blake Garris, among many, many more.

Additional thanks goes out to all the stores who supported us, especially Corner Store Comics and Collector's Corner for hosting Morbius signings. Another big thank you goes to two guys we were extremely lucky to have on board, giving this whole thing a nice consistent look, Clayton Cowles on lettering and Antonio Fabela. Big thanks goes out to Stephen Wacker for making this all possible, as well as Devin Lewis and Sana Amanat for doing all that they do. As for me, I'll be kicking around Marvel on the upcoming Marvel Knights Hulk series, as well as my Image work on titles such as Intergalactic with Ken Garing, Null/Void with James Harvey and even more yet to be announced. For now, Dr. Morbius, it's been real. Sorry for all the horrible things we put you through, but it was a pretty damn good time.

Joe Keatinge
23rd August 2013

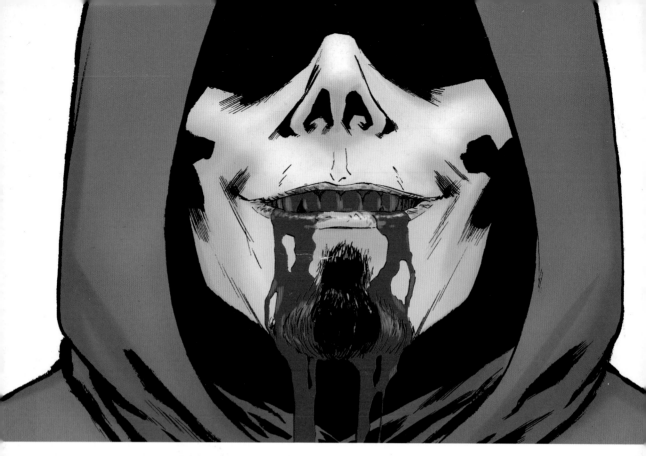

THE CREATORS

A huge **Spider-Man** fan, and winner of the 2010 Eisner Award for Best Anthology with *Popgun*, **Joe Keatinge** worked on *Savage Dragon* with **Erik Larsen**, who then hired Keatinge when he became publisher at Image Comics. The American writer went on to create extensively for Image, on titles such as *Stellar*, *Flavor*, *Glory* and *Evolution*. As well as *Morbius: The Living Vampire*, Keatinge's work for Marvel includes *What If? Age of Ultron*, *Avengers: Earth's Mightiest Heroes* and the *Marvel Knights: Hulk* miniseries, while his DC credits include *Adventures of Superman*, *DC Universe Presents* and the *Batman Incorporated Special*.

Rich Elson is a veteran of the industry, having worked in comics since the late 1980s when his artwork appeared in the pages of *2000 AD*. As well as working for publishers in his native UK, Elson has drawn *Marvel Zombies Return*, *Revolutionary War*, *Thor* and *Journey into Mystery* for the House of Ideas.

Co-creator of Image Comics' *Bitch Planet*, Canadian artist **Valentine De Landro** has created illustrations for some of comics' best publishers in the last 15 years, including Marvel (*Marvel Knights: 4*, *X-Factor*, *Thunderbolts*, *Spider-Man Loves Mary Jane*), Dark Horse (*Prometheus: Fire and Stone Omega*), Devil's Due Publishing (*GI Joe: Declassified*) and Valiant (*Shadowman*).